Travelling
SOLO
to India

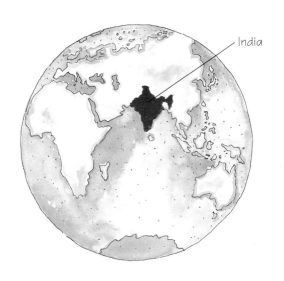

India

Written and illustrated
by Bettina Guthridge

SOLOS

KT-145-086

Southwood Books Limited
4 Southwood Lawn Road
London N6 5SF

First published in Australia by Omnibus Books 2000
This edition published in the UK under licence from
Omnibus Books by
Southwood Books Limited, 2001.

This edition produced for The Book People Ltd.,
Hall Wood Avenue, Haydock, St Helens WA11 9UL

Text and illustrations copyright © Bettina Guthridge 2000

Cover design by Lyn Mitchell
Typeset by Clinton Ellicott, Adelaide
Printed in Singapore

ISBN 1 903207 39 8

All rights reserved. No part of this publication may be
reproduced, stored in or introduced into a retrieval system,
or transmitted in any form or by any means, (electronic,
mechanical, photocopying, recording or otherwise), without
the prior written permission of both the copyright holder
and the publisher.

INDIA

The capital is New Delhi.

The money is the rupee.

1 billion (1000 million) people live in India.

The main languages are Hindi and English.

The Indian flag.

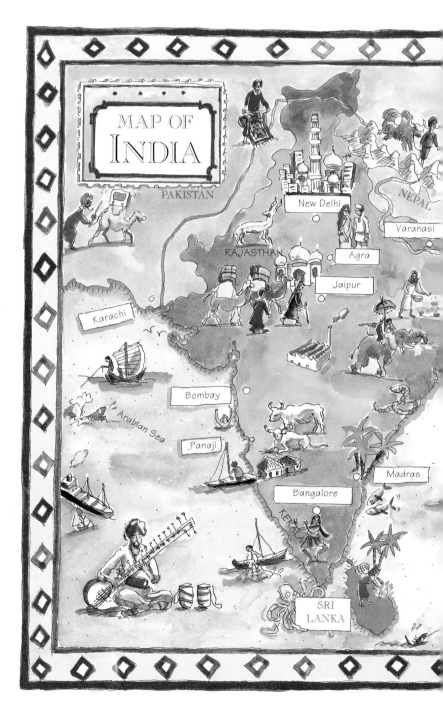

MAP OF
INDIA

PAKISTAN

New Delhi

NEPAL

Varanasi

RAJASTHAN

Agra

Jaipur

Karachi

Bombay

Arabian Sea

Panaji

Madras

Bangalore

KERALA

SRI
LANKA

CHINA
(TIBET)

Mount Everest
(8848 m)

HIMALAYAS

BHUTAN

BANGLADESH

Calcutta

MYANMAR
(BURMA)

Bay of Bengal

Andaman Islands

Nicobar Islands

N

W E

S

3

India is a country in southern Asia.
To the north are China, Nepal and
Bhutan. To the south is Sri Lanka.
Pakistan is to the west. To the east are
Bangladesh and Myanmar (Burma).

There is sea around
most of India. The
Arabian Sea is to
the west, and the
Bay of Bengal is to
the east.

In India, there are deserts, hot, wet jungles and great river plains.

In summer, India is very hot. In some places there is a lot of rain.

At the top of India are the Himalayas. These are the highest mountains in the world. They are covered in snow.

The River Ganges flows down from the Himalayas to the Bay of Bengal.

Many Indians are farmers. They need
water from the rivers to grow food.
The soil along the Ganges is rich and
there are many crops.

The monsoon brings very heavy rain to India. The name comes from the Arabic word *mausim*. It means "season". The monsoon brings the rainy season to India.

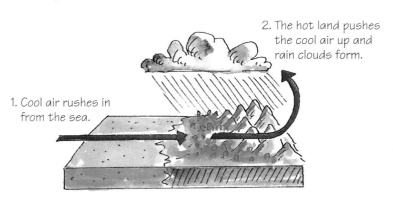

1. Cool air rushes in from the sea.

2. The hot land pushes the cool air up and rain clouds form.

The monsoon is formed like this.

Sometimes there is too much rain. The rivers flood, killing animals and crops. Many people have died in these floods.

India is the world's second most crowded country after China.

Every sixth person in the world is Indian.

As you travel across India, everything changes.

There are many different groups of people in India. Each group has its own religion, customs and language.

India has old cities and modern buildings. Some people are very wealthy, but most Indians are very poor. They farm the land for their food.

There is not much work in the country, and so many Indians go and live in the cities.

Millions of children live on the streets. Some work at the rubbish dump, picking up paper and plastic to sell. It takes all day to make enough money to buy some food.

In the small villages in the country
people live close together and help
each other. There is always work to do.

Poorer Indians build houses out of mud and sticks. The roof frame is made with bamboo and covered with palm leaves. The walls and floor are of thick mud baked dry by the sun.

mud walls

bamboo frame

roof made of palm leaves

Mud brick houses can be rebuilt easily when they are damaged in floods or storms.

dried meat

rice bin

baby cot

bedding

brass pots

wooden trunk

water jars

Inside the houses there are wooden trunks, coconut oil lamps, a bin for rice, water jars and brass pots and pans for cooking.

In the desert state of Rajasthan houses are made from cow dung, mud and chopped straw. They are decorated with paintings.

The walls of the houses are covered in mud.

Dried cow dung is sold at the market for fuel.

TEETH SELLER

SNAKE CHARMER

POTTER

FORTUNE TELLER

EAR CLEANER

SHOE SHINER

This young girl is having her face painted with a colour called *henna*.

Because the cities are so crowded, many Indians work on the street. Here you can have your ears cleaned or buy some second hand false teeth.

Anyone who can, works.

Many families are so poor that their children must work instead of going to school.

In India, even small children work in factories all day.

Children from richer families work hard at school to get good jobs.

Rich children go to school by taxi. Poor children walk to school.

In the country, schools are hard to get to as there is often no transport. Sometimes there are not enough classrooms.

In Kerala on the coast children travel to school by boat along the canals.

There are many different languages in India. Hindi and English are the languages used most.

There are more than 800 newspapers. These are printed in many languages.

Indian languages are written in many different ways.

The Hindi language is written in a special way.

These words are written in Hindi. They mean "people and places".

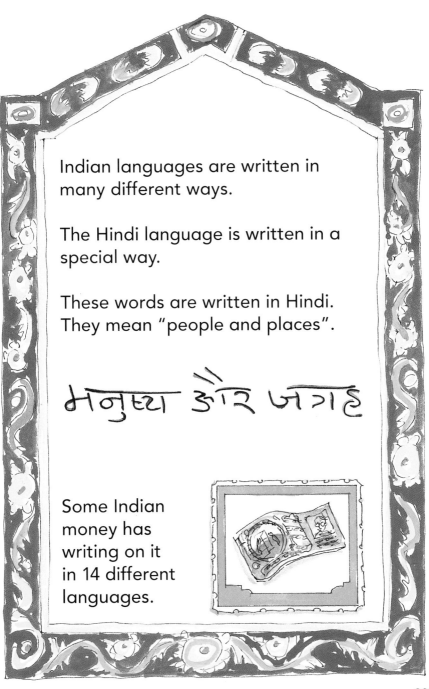

मनुष्य और जगह

Some Indian money has writing on it in 14 different languages.

There are not many cars in India. Most people are too poor to own a car.

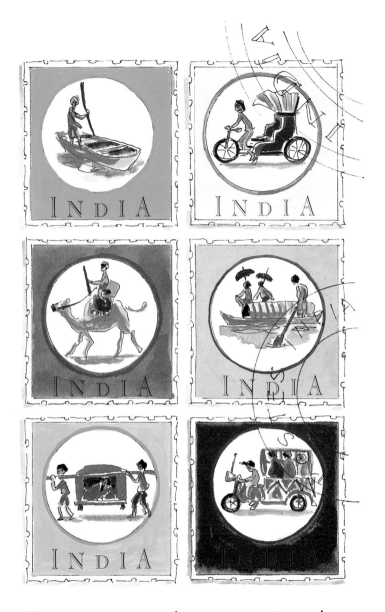

There are many other ways to travel
around.

In India, it is cheap to travel by train.

Trains are very crowded and never run on time. Lots of people must share a compartment. Sometimes trains are many hours late.

Some people travel on the roof. This costs nothing.

The Toy Train is a famous train that runs through the Himalayas on a narrow track.

Hindu gods have many different forms.

Buddhists worship the Buddha, a wise and gentle teacher.

Muslims pray to Allah.

Sikhs never cut their hair. They roll it up under their turban.

Many religions of the world can be found in India.

Most Indians are Hindus. You cannot decide to be a Hindu. To be a Hindu, you must be born into a Hindu family.

Christians worship God in their churches.

The Jewish name for God is *Yahweh*.

Some Jains wear a mask so that they will not inhale any small insects.

Parsis worship fire in their temples.

Sadhus are holy men who own nothing and must beg for food.

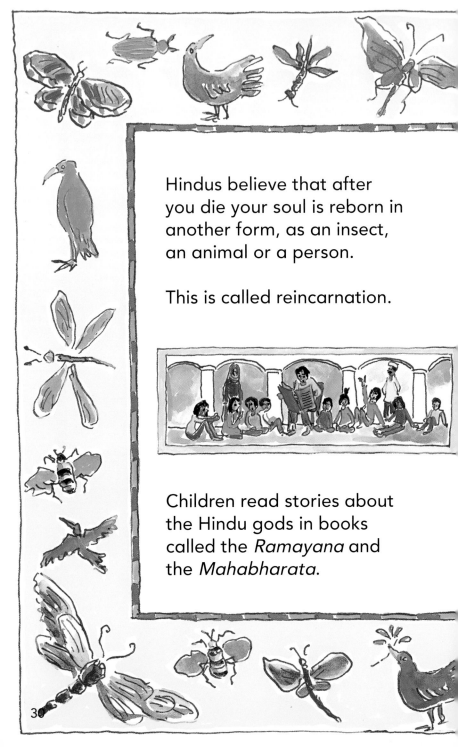

Hindus believe that after you die your soul is reborn in another form, as an insect, an animal or a person.

This is called reincarnation.

Children read stories about the Hindu gods in books called the *Ramayana* and the *Mahabharata*.

There are many Hindu gods. Brahma, Vishnu and Shiva are the chief gods. These gods take many forms.

Shiva is often shown as Lord of the Dance.

To the Hindus, all rivers are special.
The Ganges is the most special of all.
Hindus call it "Mother".

Varanasi, a beautiful city on the Ganges, is a special place for the Hindus. They believe it is lucky to die there.

There are fires all day and all night burning bodies along the river.

The ashes are scattered on the water.

The bull

The elephant

The peacock

The snake

The swan

All animals are sacred to the Hindus. Many Hindu gods take the form of animals. Because of this, Hindus do not eat meat.

The white cow is special to Hindus.
Cows wander the streets eating from
the fruit and vegetable stalls. Even
poor shop keepers do not mind.

Hindus know their place in society. They are born into one of many groups called castes.

Four of these groups are the priests, the soldiers, the merchants, and the farmers.

The priest

The soldier

The merchant
or craftsperson

The farmer

Some Hindus do not belong to a caste.
They are the "untouchables".

Other Hindus look
down on them
and they do the
dirty jobs.

In modern India,
this is changing.

The Hindus worship many gods.
Ganesha is the elephant god.
Hindus ask him to help them.

In India there are many festivals.
Some of these are *Raksha Bandhan*,
Holi, *Diwali* and *Dussehra*.

Sisters tie bracelets
around the wrists of
their brothers.

People dance
through the street
scattering water
and red powder.

For the festival of
light, tiny oil lamps are
lit in houses. Children
let off fireworks and
give away sweets.

This is a big festival
to celebrate the
defeat of the
ten-headed demon.

Most Hindu homes
have a small altar
to the gods.

Most villages have fairs. There are cock fights, magic shows, puppets, music and dancing.

At the camel fair in Rajasthan there are dancing bears and snake charmers.

Babur   Humayun   Akbar

India was once ruled by a family of
princes called the Great Moguls.

Jahangir   Shah Jahan   Aurangzeb

They were fierce warriors who loved music, painting and dancing.

They lived in splendid palaces.
These princes wore fine clothes and had many servants.

The tomb is made of white marble and precious stones.

minaret covered with white tiles

90 TAJ MAHAL 90

The Moguls built many beautiful buildings. The most famous is the Taj Mahal.

Shah Jahan built the Taj Mahal as a tomb for his wife.

It took 20 000 men 18 years to build the Taj Mahal.

Akbar's tomb

Hindu Temple

Jama Masjid
Mosque

Sikh Temple

Amer fortress

Taj-ul-Masajid
Mosque

India has many forts, temples and
mosques.

Traders from many countries once came to India.

The traders of the British East India Company ruled India for many years. They bought goods cheaply to sell back home. These traders treated the Indian people badly.

The British Government took over the country and built railways and schools.

The British changed India. Their way of life can still be seen in India today.

India is famous for its tigers and elephants. There are not many left now.

The Moguls loved to hunt. They killed many wild animals. Today there are reserves to protect the animals that are left.

Fishermen in tiger reserves wear "face" masks on the back of their heads. This keeps tigers away. A tiger will not come near if it sees your eyes watching it.

Bright colours are everywhere in India.

They can be seen in the temple
paintings, and in the clothes and crafts.

During festivals, even the cows' horns are painted in bright colours.

Most of the time it is very hot in India,
and so clothes must be cool.

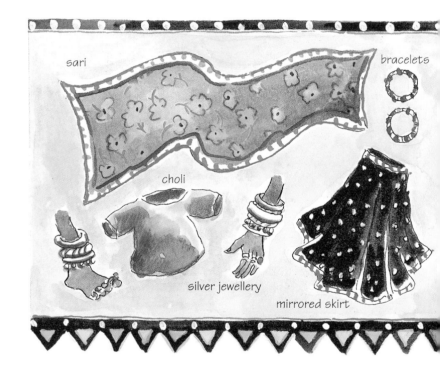

sari

bracelets

choli

silver jewellery

mirrored skirt

Many women
wear a *sari*.
This is a long
piece of cloth.
It is wrapped
around the body
many times.

Many men wear shirts and suits. Others wear a shirt without a collar (a *kurta*) over trousers or a loincloth (a *dhoti*).

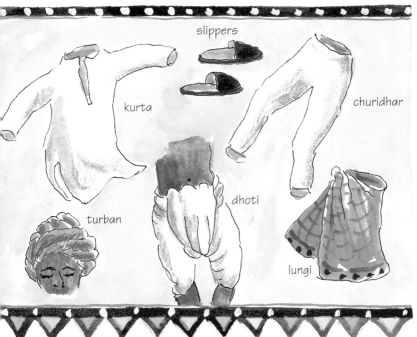

slippers

kurta

churidhar

dhoti

turban

lungi

Children wear Indian clothes or T-shirts and shorts.

Many men wear turbans.

The food in India can be hot.
Indians like to eat curry,
a stew made with spices
and chilli.

Hindus eat vegetable curries.
Curry can be made with
fish, meat or eggs as well.

Sometimes a meal is served
on a big banana leaf.

Chapatis are a
flat bread made
of wheat or millet
flour. They are
served with most
meals.

A *thali* is a metal tray with
bowls of curry and
vegetables.

Rice and a bread called
chapati are served with curry.

A side dish made with yogurt
helps cool down a hot curry!

Indians love singing and dancing.
The *sitar*, the *tamboura* and the *tabla*
are heard at every festival and
wedding, or in the market place.

In Rajasthan the music is famous.

Special songs are written for the *Diwali* and *Holi* festivals.

The monks of the Digambara sect in India wear no clothes.

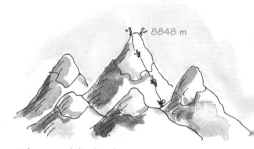

8848 m

The world's highest mountain is Mount Everest in the Himalayas.

When Indians greet each other they do not shake hands. They put their palms together and bow their heads slightly.

The wettest place on earth is Cherrapunji in India. It has 11 500 mm (450 inches) of rain each year.

India makes more films every year than any other country in the world. The films are made in Bombay. Sometimes Bombay is called "Bollywood".

Know?

The Mogul prince Akbar loved his elephant very much. When it died, he built a tomb for it.

A *fakir* is a holy man. Some *fakirs* bury themselves up to the neck in sand to make up for their sins. Sometimes people give them money.

It is thought that one tiger is killed every day in India. Parts of the body are used to make medicine.

The Indian railways are the biggest employer in the world. Nearly 1 700 000 people work for the railways.

GLOSSARY

Allah ★ the Muslim name for God.

altar ★ place for making offerings to a god.

brass ★ a kind of metal.

canal ★ water way that has been dug to carry people and goods between two places.

caste ★ a group that a Hindu is born into.

cock fight ★ fight between two male birds.

compartment ★ "room" in a train where passengers sit.

customs ★ ways of doing things that people share.

dung ★ animal droppings.

festival ★ a time to celebrate and have fun.

flood ★ a flow over of water from a river on to land.

fortress ★ building to protect people.

fortune teller ★ someone who is paid to tell the future.

fuel ★ something that is burnt to make heat or power.

henna ★ red dye used to draw patterns or to colour hair.

market ★ place for buying and selling goods.

minaret ★ tall, thin tower of a mosque.

Moguls ★ powerful rulers from a long time ago.

monsoon ★ wind in southern Asia that brings heavy rain.

mosque ★ place where Muslims worship.

mud brick ★ brick made from mud, dried in the sun.

palace ★ grand home for a king or ruler.

reincarnation ★ the belief that people can come back as a different creature after they die.

sadhu ★ man who devotes himself to a religious life.

second hand ★ something that has been used before.

sitar ★ musical instrument with strings.

snake charmer ★ man who keeps a snake in a basket and makes it "dance" to the music he plays.

tabla ★ drum.

tamboura ★ musical instrument with strings.

temple ★ place to worship.

tomb ★ grand building made around a grave to honour a special person after he or she has died.

INDEX